Better Drums W... Rockschool

Welcome to Drums Grade 5	2
Drum Notation Explained	3

Pieces:

Radioheads	4
Mud Pie	6
Downtime	8
Queen For A Day	10
In The Bag	12
Rock Steady	14

Technical Exercises	16
Sight Reading	18
Improvisation & Interpretation	18
Ear Tests	19
General Musicianship Questions	20
The Guru's Guide	21

A *Rockschool* Publication
Broomfield House, Broomfield Road, Richmond, Surrey TW9 3HS

Welcome To *Drums* Grade 5

Welcome to the Rockschool *Drums* Grade 5 pack. The book and CD contain everything needed to play drums in this grade. The CD has full stereo mixes of each tune and backing tracks to play along with for practice. Handy tips on playing the pieces and the marking schemes can be found in the Guru's Guide on page 21. If you have any queries about this or any other Rockschool exam, please call us on **020 8332 6303** or email us at office@rockschool.co.uk or visit our website http://www.rockschool.co.uk. Good luck!

Performer Zone Techniques in Grade 4 and Grade 5

The eight Rockschool grades are divided into four Zones. *Drums* Grade 5, along with Grade 4, is part of the *Performer Zone*. This Zone is for those of you who are confident in all the key skills on drums and who are stepping up to more advanced skills and stylistic expression.

Grade 4: in this grade you use a range of physical and expressive techniques with confidence, including accented notes within phrases, rimshots, crushed notes and the extension of basic rudiments into fills and patterns. You are also experimenting with a range of dynamics from very quiet (*pp*) to very loud (*ff*). It is in this grade that you are continuing to develop your ability to play with stylistic authority.

Grade 5: as a player you will be confident in a whole range of physical and expressive techniques, including hi hat foot techniques, the use of 'ghosting' to shape rhythmic groups and the incorporation of more sophisticated rudiments as part of your playing. You will be able to demonstrate your abilities across a range of styles.

Performer Zone Drums Exams

There are **three** types of exam that can be taken using this pack: Grade Exam, Performance Certificate and Band Exam.

- ***Drums* Grade 5 Exam: this is for players who want to develop performance and technical skills**

Players wishing to enter for a *Drums* Grade 5 exam need to prepare **three** pieces, of which **one** may be a free choice piece chosen from outside the printed repertoire. In addition, you must prepare the technical exercises in this book, undertake either a sight reading test or an improvisation & interpretation test, take an ear test and answer general musicianship questions. Samples of these are printed in the book.

- ***Performer Zone* Performance Certificate in Drums: this is for players who want to focus on performing in a range of styles**

To enter for your *Performer Zone* Performance Certificate you play pieces only. You can choose any **five** of the six tunes printed in this book, or you can bring in up to **two** free choice pieces as long as they meet the standards set out in the Guru's Guide below.

- ***Performer Zone* Band Exam in Guitar, Bass and Drums: this is for players who want to play as a band**

The *Performer Zone* Band Exam is for all of you who are in a group, and features guitar, bass and drums. You play together in the exam, using the parts printed in the Guitar, Bass and Drum books. Like the *Performer Zone* Performance Certificate, you can play **five** of the six printed pieces, or you can include up to **two** free choice pieces as long as they meet the standards set out in the Guru's Guide below. If you take this exam you will be marked as a unit with each player expected to contribute equally to the overall performance of each piece played.

Drum Notation Explained

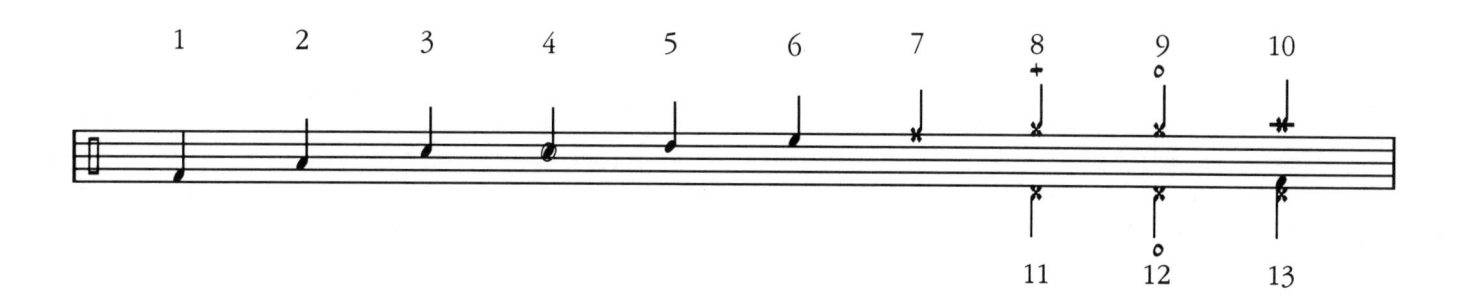

1. Kick drum
2. Floor tom
3. Snare drum
4. Rim shot
5. Medium tom
6. High tom
7. Ride cymbal
8. Hi hat closed
9. Hi hat open
10. Crash cymbal
11. Hi hat (foot)
12. Hi hat open (foot)
13. Hi hat & kick drum together

General Musical Notation

Accent: Accentuate note (play it louder)

Accent: Accentuate note with great intensity

Repeat Bars: Repeat the bars between the repeat indications.

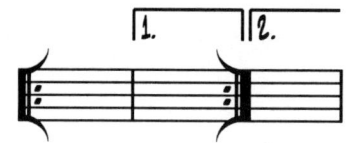

1st and 2nd Time Repeat Endings: When a repeated section has different endings, play the 1st ending only the 1st time, and the 2nd ending only the second time.

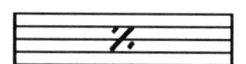

1 Bar Repeat: Repeat previous bar. In higher grades these may also be marked *sim*.

2 Bar Repeat: Repeat the previous 2 bars. In higher grades these may also be marked *sim*.

Da Capo Al Fine: Go back to the beginning of the song and play until the bar marked FINE (end).

Dal Segno Al Coda: Go back to the sign (𝄋), then play until the bar marked TO CODA ✚ then skip to the section marked ✚ CODA.

Radioheads

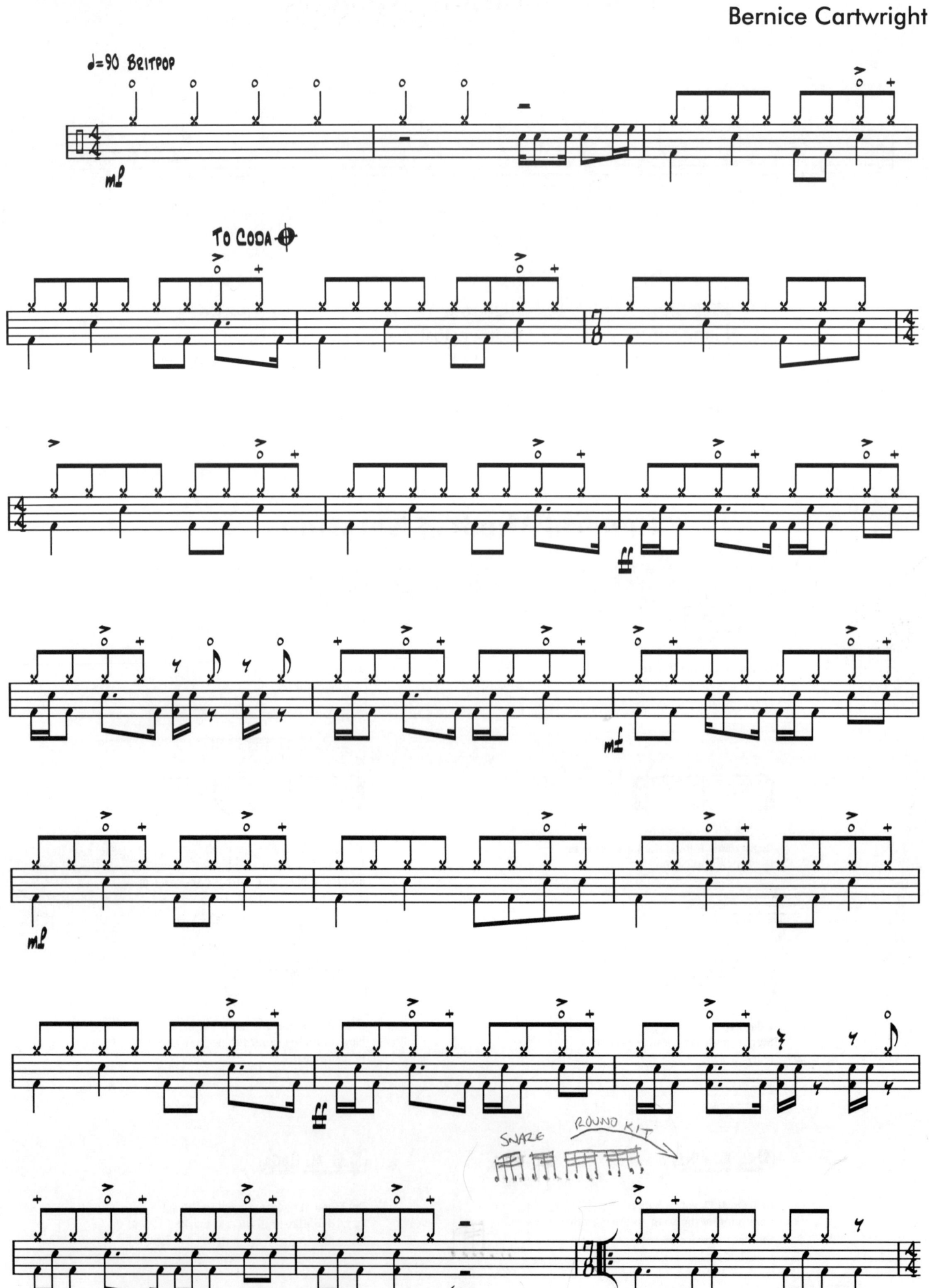

Bernice Cartwright

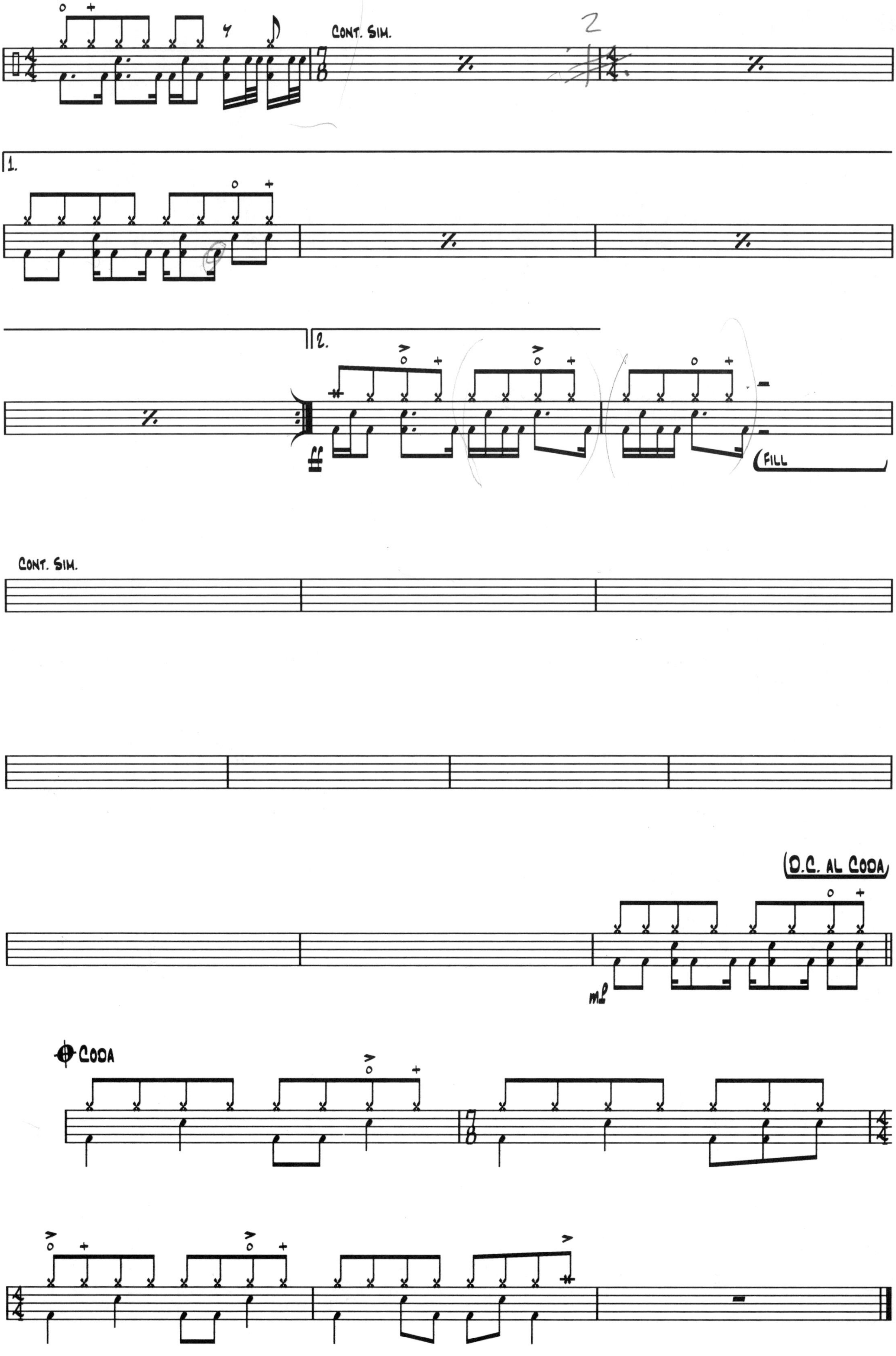
CONT. SIM.
1.
2.
ff
FILL
CONT. SIM.
D.C. AL CODA
mf
CODA

Mud Pie

Hussein Boon

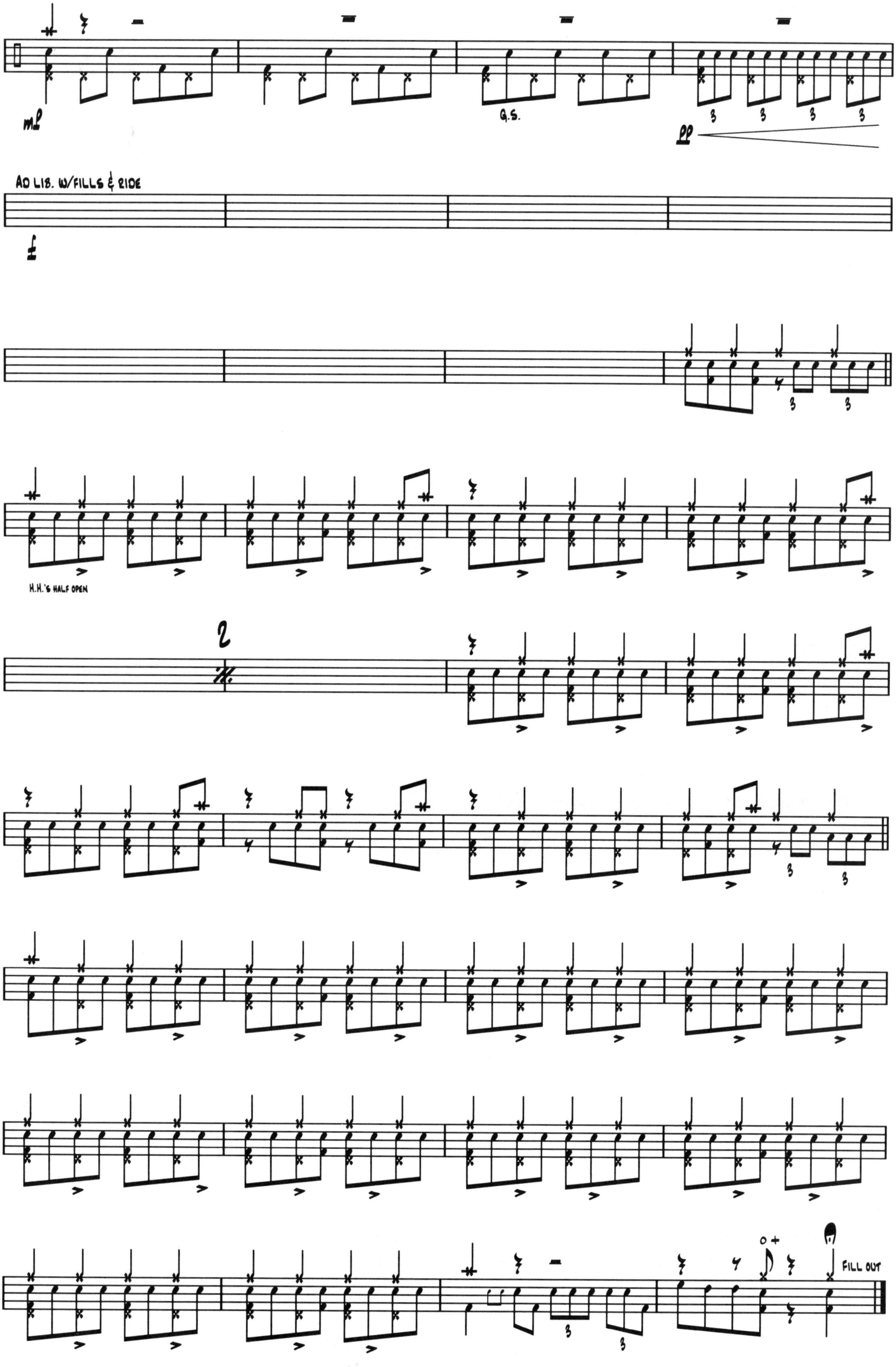
mf
G.S.
pp
AD LIB. W/FILLS & RIDE
f
H.H.'s HALF OPEN
FILL OUT

Downtime

Hussein Boon

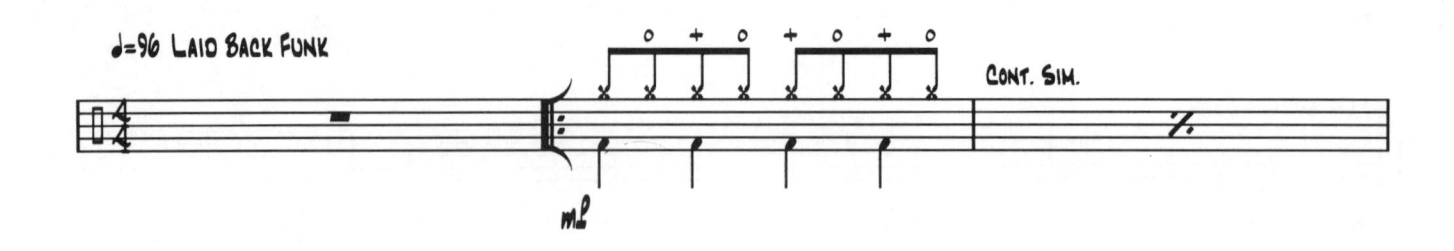

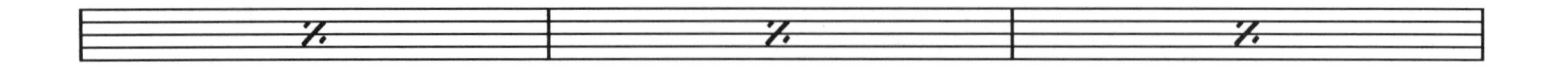

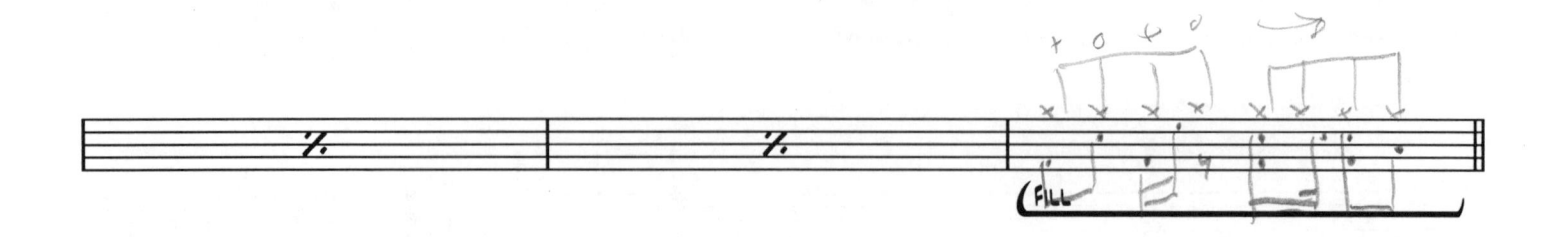

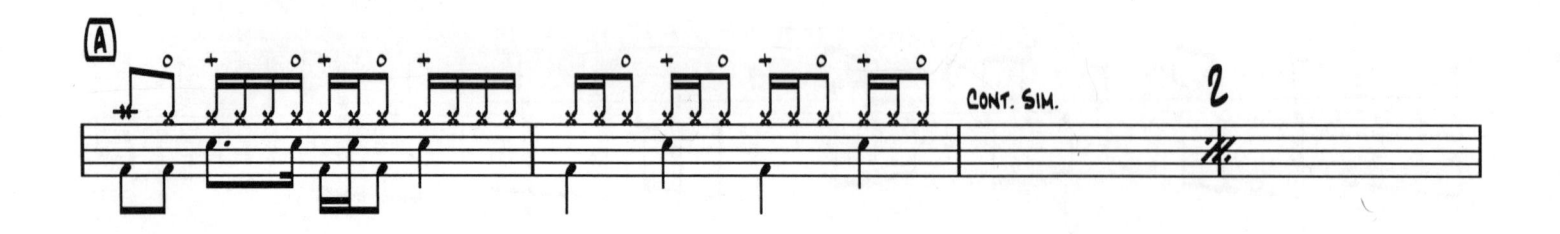

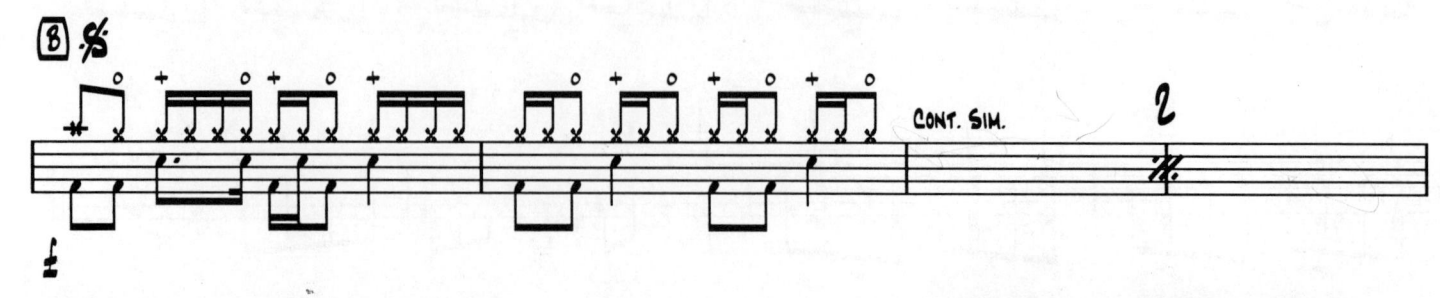

© 1998 by Rock School Ltd.

This music is copyright. Photocopying is illegal

To Coda
2
Fill
C
mf
Cont. Sim.
2
2
f
D
mp
D.S. al Coda
Cresc. poco a poco
Fill
Coda
Cymbals ad lib.

Queen For A Day

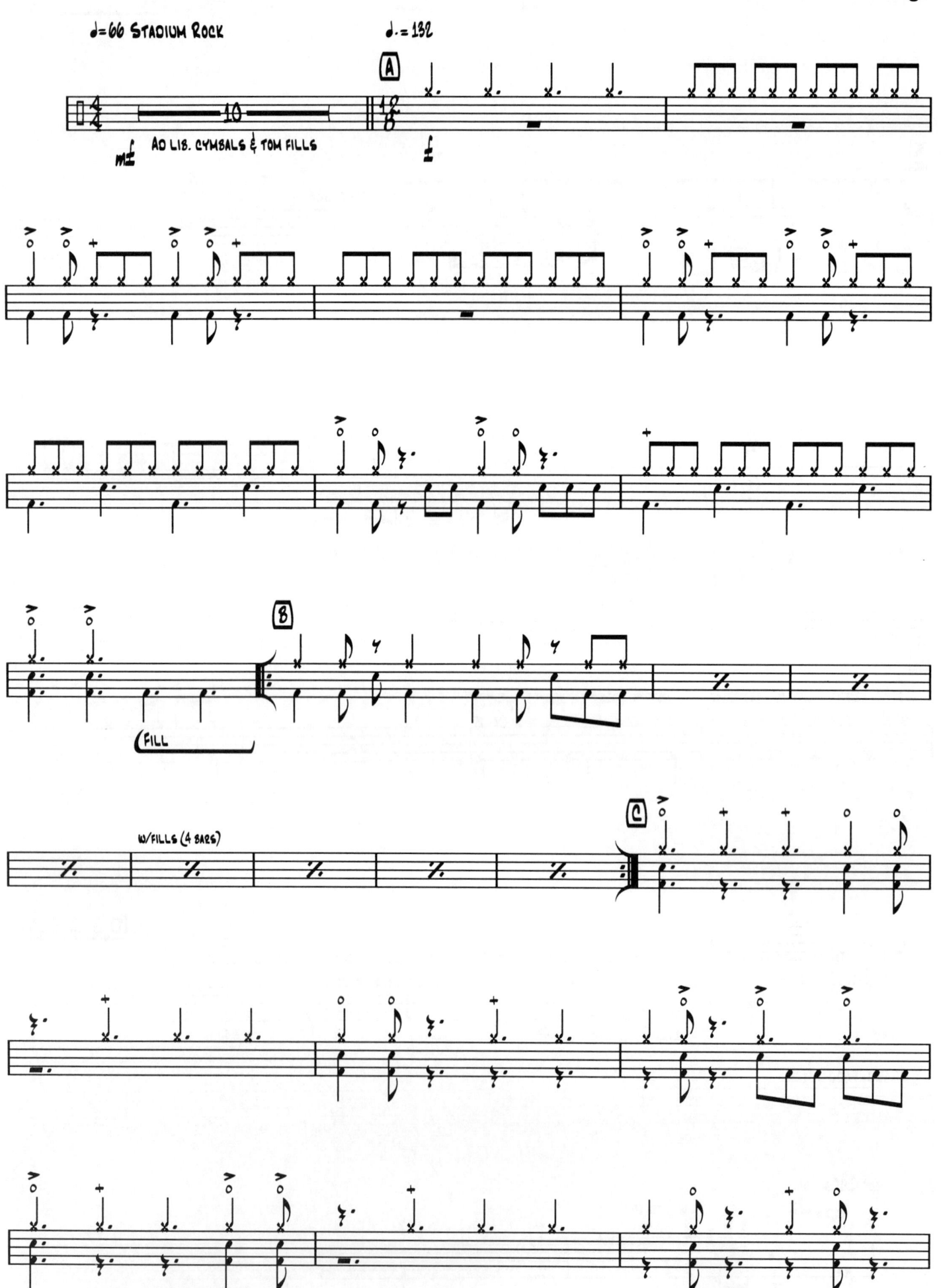

Deirdre Cartwright

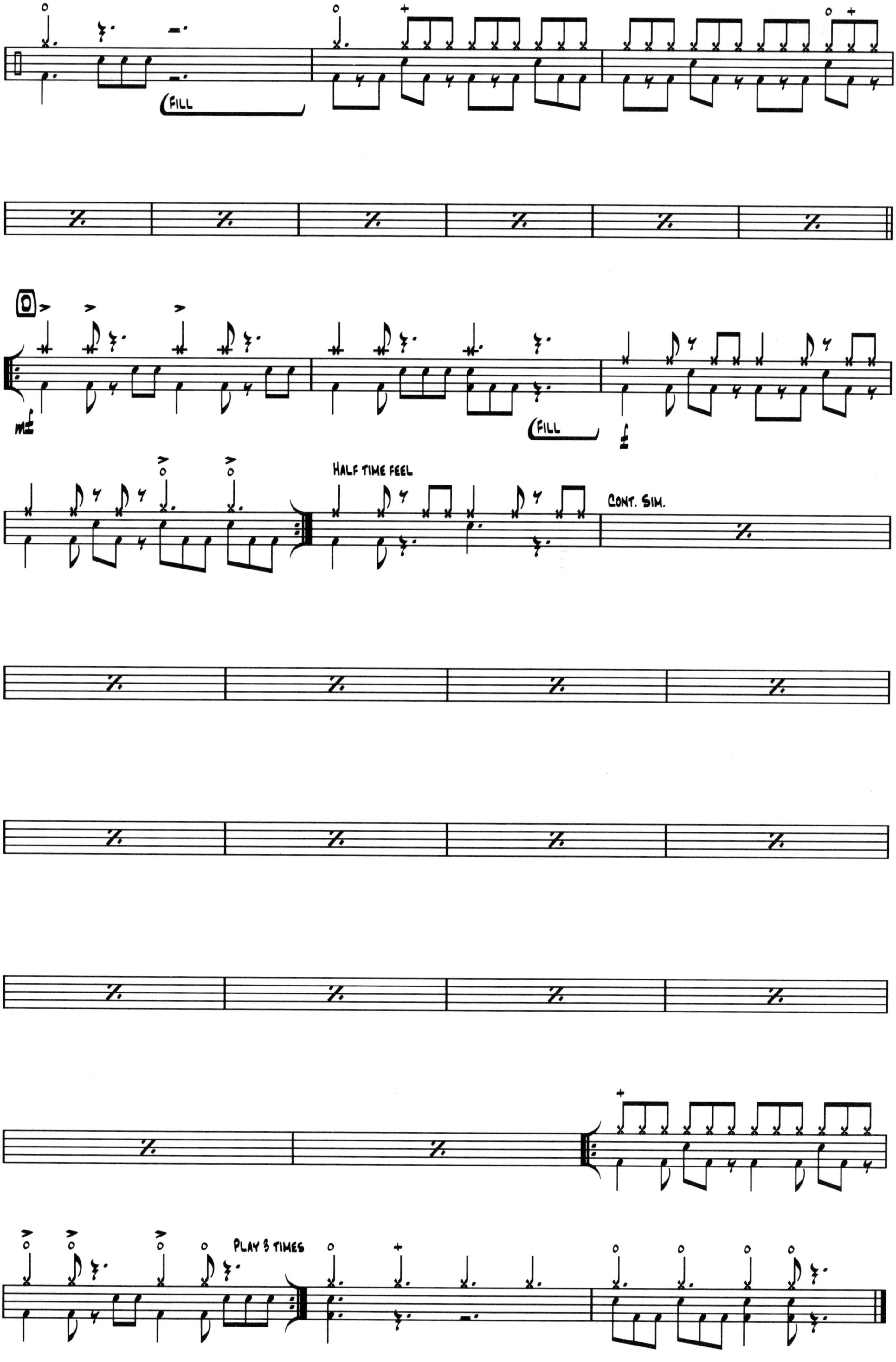
FILL
D
mf
FILL
f
HALF TIME FEEL
CONT. SIM.
PLAY 3 TIMES

In The Bag

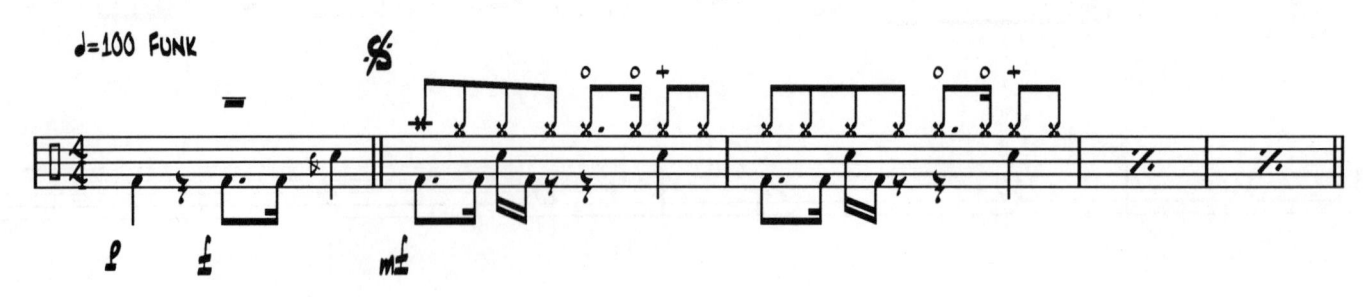

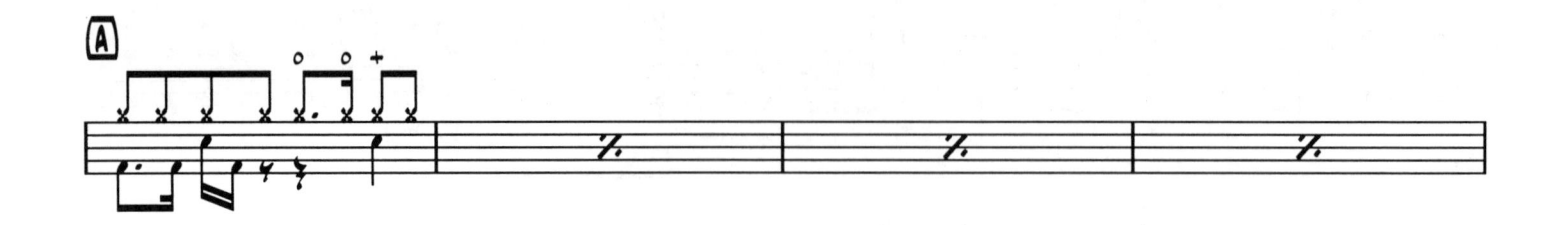

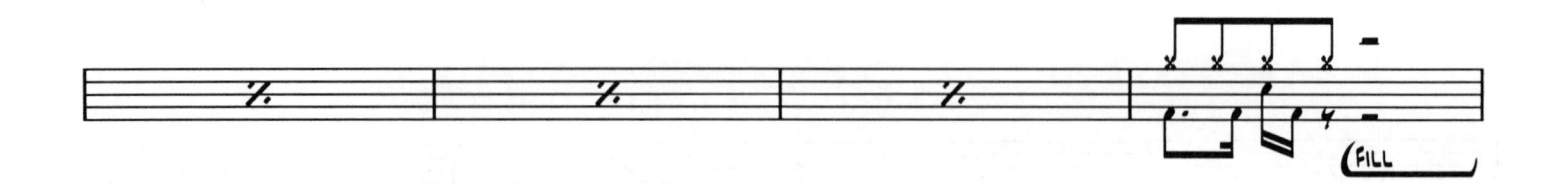

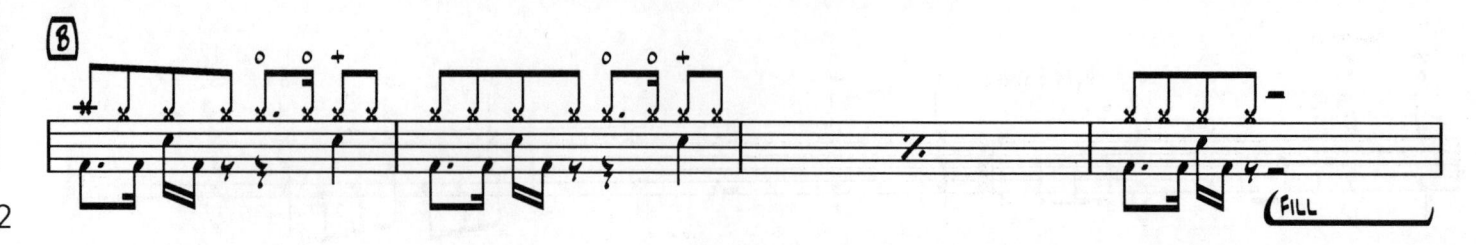

Steve Wrigley

© 1998 by Rock School Ltd.

FILL
D
E
F
DRUM BREAK - OPEN OUT ON GROOVE
x4
D.S. AL CODA
G
R/C BELL
1. 2. 3.
4.
FILL
CODA

Rock Steady

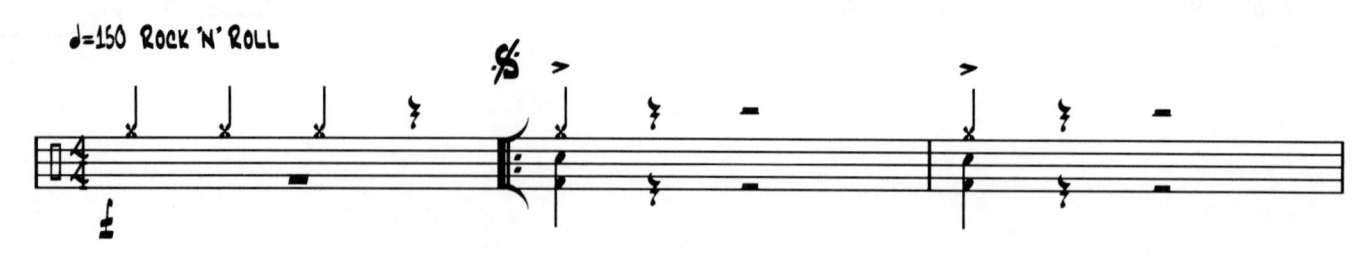

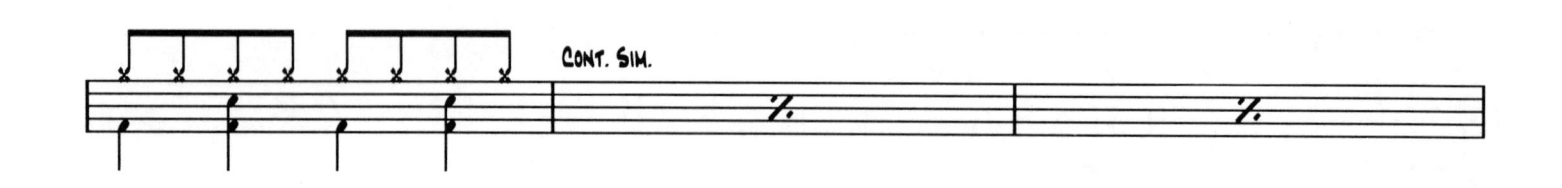

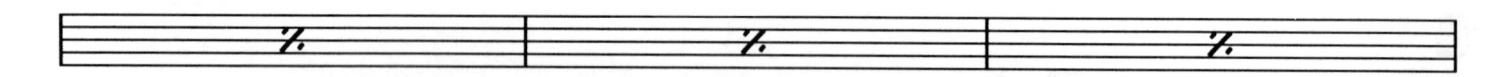

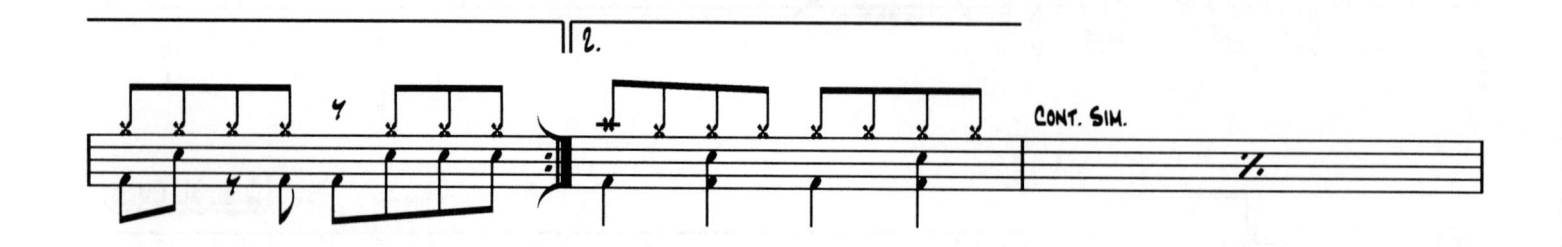

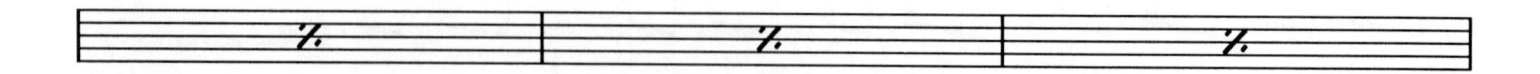

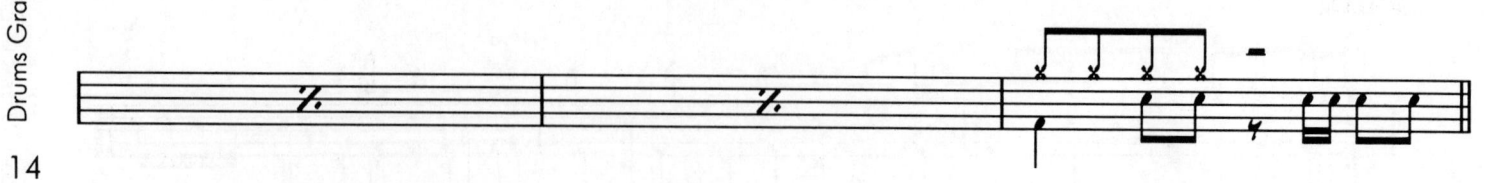

Dave Barnard

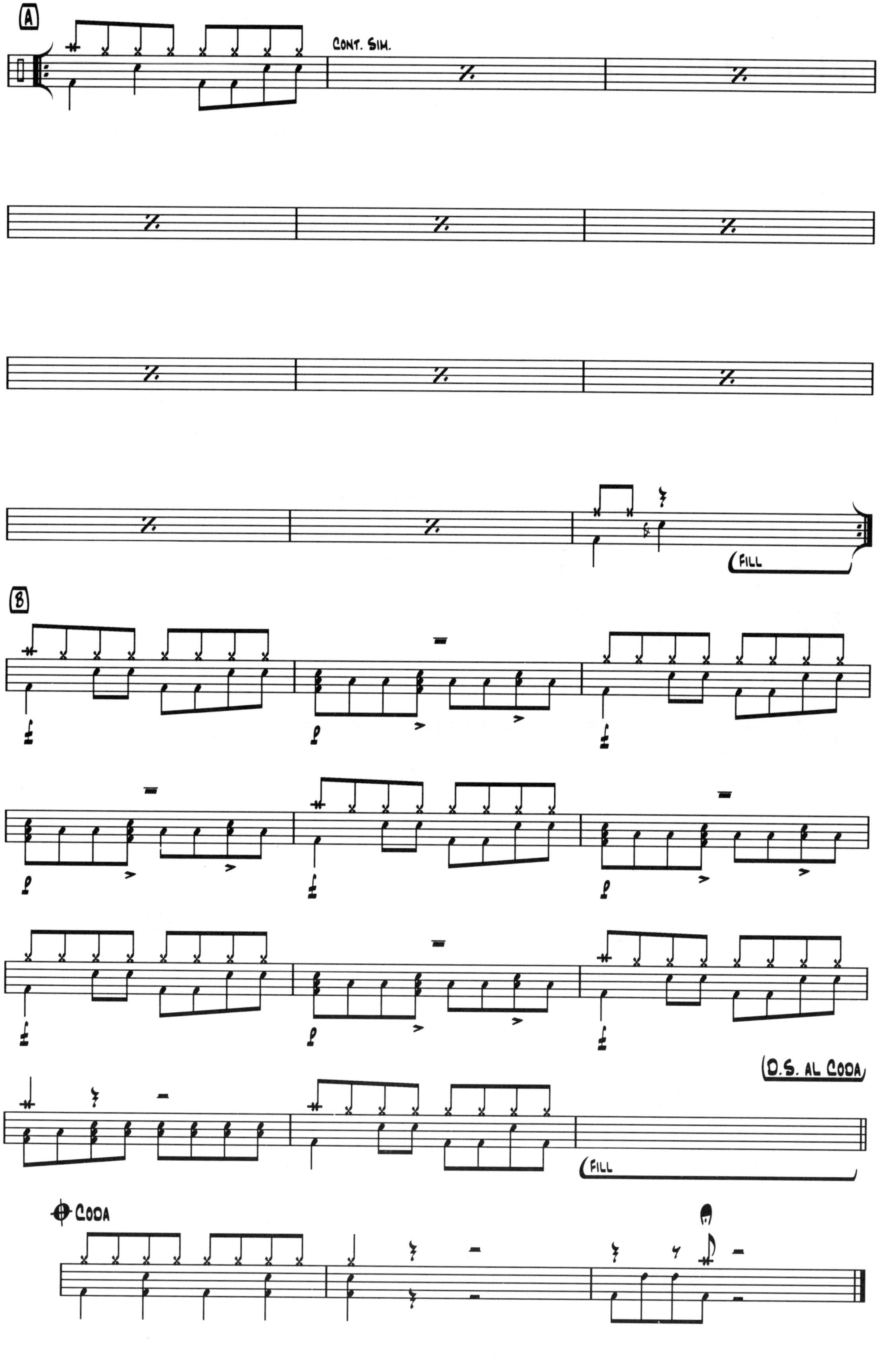
A
CONT. SIM.
FILL
B
D.S. AL CODA
FILL
CODA

Technical Exercises

In this section, the examiner will ask you to play a selection of exercises drawn from each of the five groups shown below. You do not need to memorise the exercises (and can use the book in the exam) but the examiner will be looking for the speed of your response. The examiner will also give credit for the level of your musicality.

The L and F markings shown underneath the notes represent the sticking patterns: leading hand and following hand.

Group A: Single and double strokes ♩ = 80

You will be asked to play this group of three exercises as a continuous sequence (including the repeats as shown), in either single or double strokes. The examples shown below are in single strokes.

a) In 8th notes

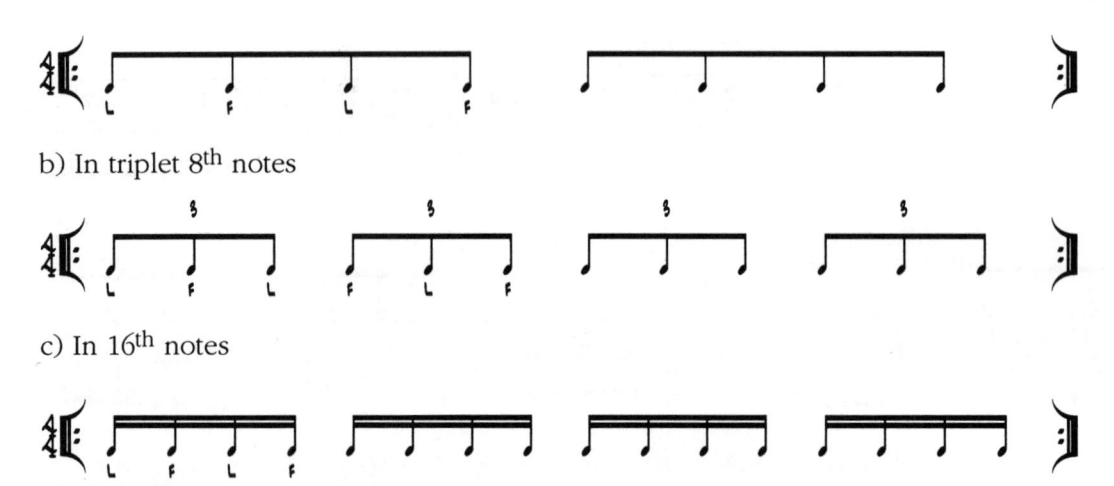

b) In triplet 8th notes

c) In 16th notes

Group B: Paradiddles ♩ = 80

a) Standard Paradiddle in 16th notes

b) Inverted Paradiddle in 16th notes

c) Inverted Paradiddle in 16th notes with displaced accents

Group C: Rolls ♩ = 80

a) Five stroke roll

b) Seven stroke roll

Group D: Flams, drags and ruffs

a) Flams in quarter notes

b) Flams in triplet 8th notes

c) Drags in quarter notes

d) Ruffs in quarter notes

Group E: Triplets ♩ = 90

a) Standard triplet in 8th notes

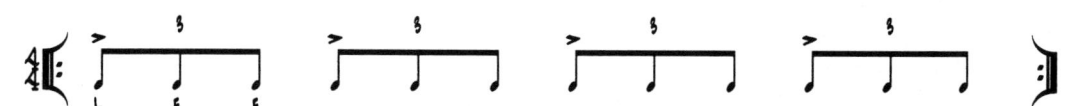

b) Reversed triplet in 8th notes

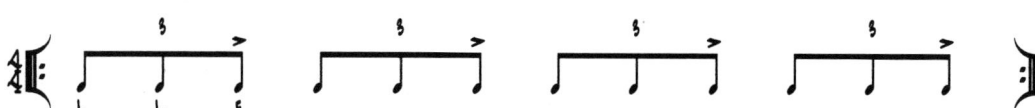

Sight Reading *or* Improvisation & Interpretation

In this section you have a choice between either a sight reading test or an improvisation & interpretation test. Printed below is an example of the type of **sight reading** test you are likely to encounter in the exam. The examiner will allow you 90 seconds to prepare it and will set the tempo for you on a metronome.

Printed below is an example of the type of **improvisation & interpretation** test you are likely to encounter in an exam. You will be asked to play an improvised groove for 12 bars in one of the following styles: blues, rock, funk or jazz. The basis of the groove to be improvised is given in the first two bars. The examiner will allow you 90 seconds to prepare it and will set the tempo for you on a metronome.

Ear Tests

You will find two ear tests in this grade. The examiner will play each test to you twice on CD.

Test 1

You will be asked to identify a drum fill made up of a number of note value combinations played on the snare drum. An example of this type of test is shown below.

Answer: (i)   one set of triplet 8th notes
(ii) one set of sextuplet 16th notes
(iii) a pair of 8th notes
(iv) a pair of 16th notes and an 8th note

Test 2

You will be asked to play back on your drums a four bar drum groove using the following drum voices: crash cymbal, hi hat, snare drum and kick drum. An example of this type of test is shown below.

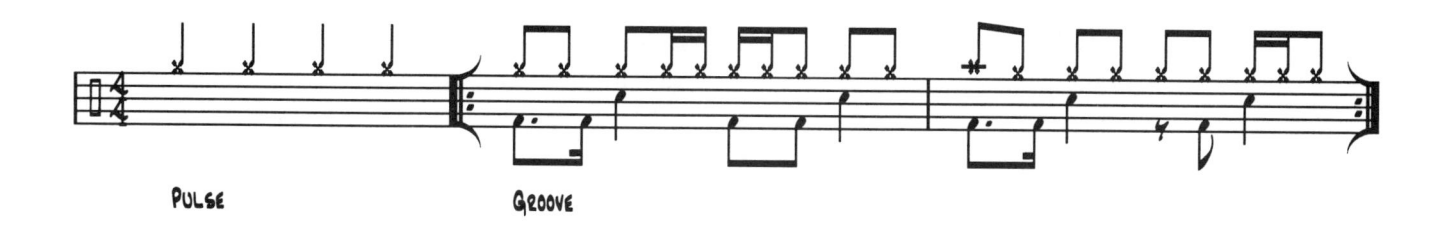

General Musicianship Questions

You will be asked five General Musicianship Questions at the end of the exam.

Topics:

i) Musical knowledge
ii) Knowledge of your instrument

The musical knowledge questions will cover the following topics at this grade:

- Any and all music signs as displayed on the staff

The instrument knowledge questions will cover the following topics at this grade:

- Names and positions of all drum voices
- Procedures for changing a snare drum head
- Procedure for tuning drums
- Recognition of main drums makes

Questions on all these topics will be based on pieces played by you in the exam

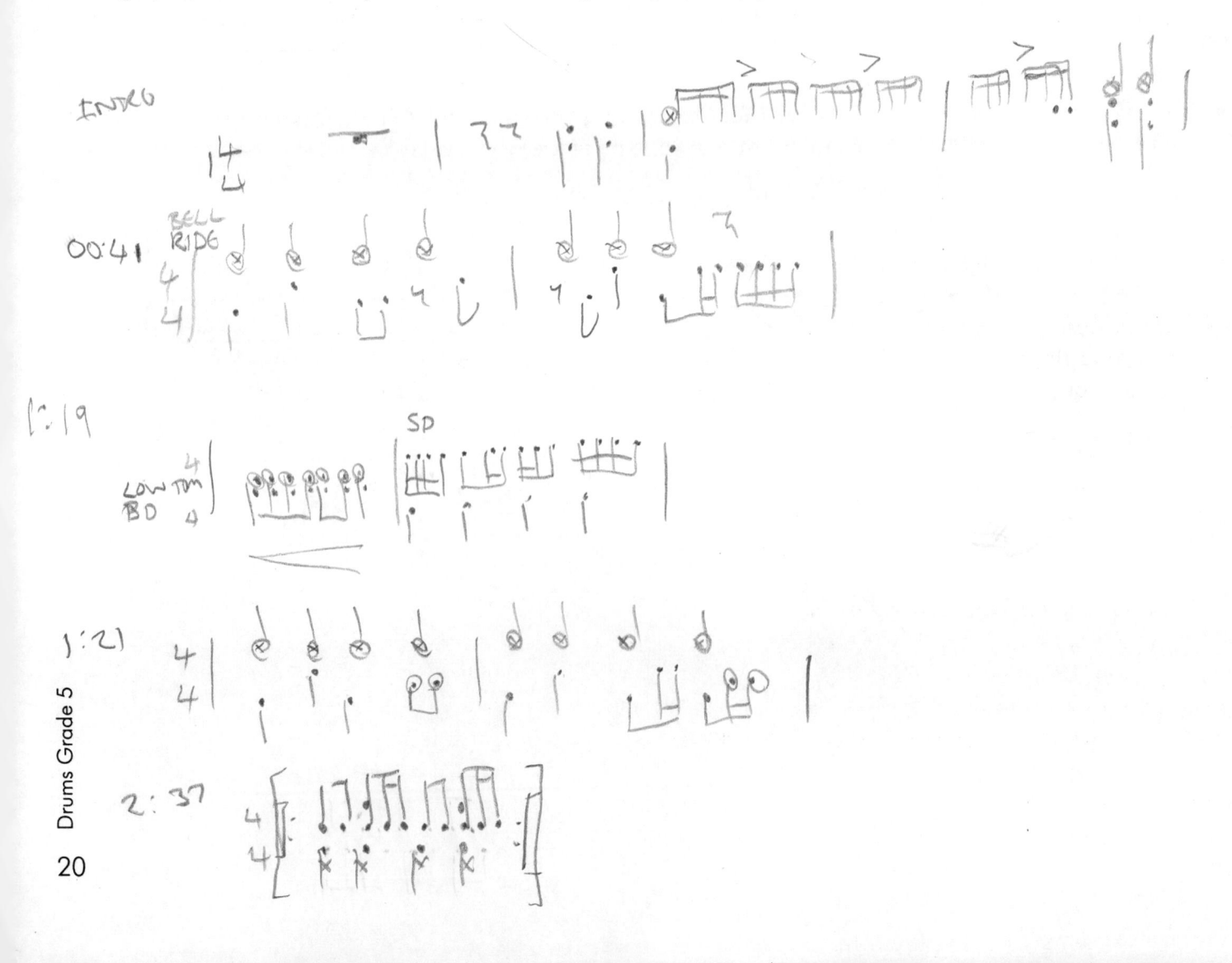

The Guru's Guide To *Drums* Grade 5

This section contains some handy hints compiled by Rockschool's Drums Guru to help you get the most out of the performance pieces. Do feel free to adapt the tunes to suit your playing style. Remember, these tunes are your chance to show your musical imagination and personality.

Care has been taken to match the printed parts to the audio performances. Where discrepancies occur, players may either follow the printed part or devise grooves and fills to suit the style as required. Please also note the solos featured in the full mixes are not meant to be indicative of the standard required for the grade.

Drums Grade 5 Tunes

Rockschool tunes help you play the hit tunes you enjoy. The pieces have been written by top pop and rock composers and players according to style specifications drawn up by Rockschool.

The tunes printed here are divided into two groups of three pieces. The first group of pieces belongs to the *contemporary mainstream* and features current styles in today's charts. The second group of pieces consists of *roots styles*, those classic grooves and genres which influence every generation of performers.

CD full mix track 1, backing track 7: *Radioheads*

Brit Pop, Radiohead style. This piece looks quite challenging and features trademark kick drum rhythms (for example bars 9 and 11). However the pulse of the piece is quite slow so take the time available to nail the part properly. You should also look to develop the part in the second half of the piece in the *cont sim* passages.

Composer: Bernice Cartwright. Bernice is a successful bass player and composer with a string of TV and theatre credits to her name.

CD full mix track 2, backing track 8: *Mud Pie**

Modern Texas blues in style of the late Stevie Ray Vaughan (check out his *Scuttlebuttin'*). Although taken at quite a lick, this shuffle rhythm is mainly straightforward with open hi hat quarter notes, triplets and driving snare rhythms in the second half. Feel free to ad lib where required and play around with the dynamics.

Composer: Hussein Boon. Hussein says he plays mainly "noisy pop" and the odd bit of drum 'n' bass. He has graced bands such as Beats International, Microgroove and De La Soul and artists such as Omar and Karen Ramirez.

CD full mix track 3, backing tack 9: *Downtime**

This is a laid back funk tune à la Jamiroquai. The opening features a simple hi hat and kick drum pattern followed by funky hi hat figures and fills. Use the passages marked *sim* to develop your own ideas within the pulse, while alternating quiet and loud dynamics to add musical colour.

Composer: Hussein Boon.

CD full mix track 4, backing track 10: *Queen for a Day*

Stadium rock in all its glory. In this piece you have a ten bar intro featuring ad lib cymbal and tom fills, before the 12/8 shuffle kicks in. The part is quite sparsely notated, particularly in the second half, leaving you free to develop an appropriate feel using different drum voices and dynamic changes.

Composer: Deirdre Cartwright. Deirdre fronted the TV *Rockschool* series in the 1980's and now plays and teachers extensively throughout Europe.

CD full mix track 5, backing track 11: *In the Bag*

James Brown's influence can be felt throughout the history of popular music from Little Richard and Prince to modern funk players and even rap artists. This piece feature a trademark funk groove played at 100 bpm. The patterns require solid control and should sound comfortable. Watch out for the fills and open out the groove for the eight bar drum break after bar 40.

Composer: Steve Wrigley: Steve is an exceptionally gifted guitarist and composer who has written a number of theatre and TV scores as well as playing for artists such as P J Proby, Bernard Purdie and Sarah Jane Morris.

CD full mix track 6, backing track 12: *Rock Steady*

A rock & roll piece in the style of Chuck Berry. This part is mainly straightforward with hi hat eighths and a four to the floor pattern with the kick drum. The [B] section features a driving toms-snare-kick drum pattern which you may adapt to suit.

Composers: Dave Barnard. Dave began his career as a punk rocker before developing a taste for Latin music. He is now bass player and MD for King Salsa and plays a lot throughout Europe.

CD Musicians:

Guitars: Deirdre Cartwright and Hussein Boon on (*) **Bass:** Geoff Gascoyne **Drums:** Mike Bradley
Keyboards and programming: Adrian York

Grade Exam Marking Scheme

The table below shows the marking scheme for the *Drums* Grade 5 exam.

ELEMENT	PASS	MERIT	DISTINCTION
Piece 1 Piece 2 Piece 3	13 out of 20 13 out of 20 13 out of 20	15 out of 20 15 out of 20 15 out of 20	17+ out of 20 17+ out of 20 17+ out of 20
Technical Exercises	11 out of 15	12 out of 15	13+ out of 15
Either: Sight Reading *Or:* Improvisation & Interpretation	6 out of 10	7 out of 10	8+ out of 10
Ear Tests	6 out of 10	7 out of 10	8+ out of 10
General Musicianship Questions	3 out of 5	4 out of 5	5 out of 5
Total Marks	**Pass: 65% +**	**Pass: 75% +**	**Pass: 85% +**

Performer Zone Performance Certificate/Band Exam Marking Scheme

The table below shows the marking scheme for both the *Performer Zone* Performance Certificate and the *Performer Zone* Band Exam. You will see that the Pass mark for both is now **70%**. The Merit mark is **80%** and the mark for a Distinction performance is **90%**.

ELEMENT	PASS	MERIT	DISTINCTION
Piece 1	14 out of 20	16 out of 20	18+ out of 20
Piece 2	14 out of 20	16 out of 20	18+ out of 20
Piece 3	14 out of 20	16 out of 20	18+ out of 20
Piece 4	14 out of 20	16 out of 20	18+ out of 20
Piece 5	14 out of 20	16 out of 20	18+ out of 20
Total Marks	**Pass: 70% +**	**Merit: 80% +**	**Distinction: 90% +**

Free Choice Song Criteria

You can bring in your own performance pieces to play in any of the exams featured. In the Grade Exams you can bring in **one** piece.

In either the *Performer Zone* Performance Certificate or the *Performer Zone* Band Exam you may bring in up to **two** pieces. You should read the following criteria carefully.

- Players may bring in either their own compositions or songs already in the public domain, including hits from the charts.
- Songs may be performed either solo or to a CD or tape backing track.
- Players should bring in two copies of the piece to be performed, notated either in standard notation, chord charts or TAB. Players must use an original copy of the tune to be performed, and must provide a second copy for the examiner, which may be a photocopy. For copyright reasons, photocopies handed to the examiner will be retained and destroyed by Rock School in due course.
- Players may perform either complete songs or extracts: such as a solo part.
- Players should aim to keep their free choice songs below 2 minutes in length.
- *Player Zone* Band Exam parts should feature independent lines for all instruments.
- Players should aim to make each free choice song of a technical standard similar to those published in the Rockschool *Drums* Grade 5 book. However, examiners will be awarding credit for how well you perform the song. In general players should aim to play songs that mix the following physical and expressive techniques and rhythm skills:

Physical Techniques: accurate and independent hand and foot co-ordination.

Expressive Techniques: use of accented notes within phrases, a wide dynamic range (very soft to very loud), fills, flams, ghosted notes within patterns, rimshots and the extension of a wide range of rudiment patterns within your playing style.

Rhythm Skills: songs should contain a mixture of whole, half, quarter, eighth and 16th notes, dotted quarter notes and their associated rests. Songs should contain simple uses of syncopation and be in 4/4 time signatures with the occasional bar of different time signatures as required.

You, or your teacher, may wish to adapt an existing piece of music to suit the criteria above. You should ensure that any changes to the music are clearly marked on the sheet submitted to the examiner.

Entering Rockschool Exams

Entering a Rockschool exam is easy, whether for the Grade, the *Performer Zone* Performance Certificate or the *Performer Zone* Band Exam. Please read through these instructions carefully before filling in the exam entry form. Information on current exam fees can be obtained from Rock School by ringing **020 8332 6303**

- You should enter for the exam of your choice when you feel ready.

- You can enter for any one of three examination periods. These are shown below with their closing dates.

PERIOD	DURATION	CLOSING DATE
Period A	1st February to 15th March	1st December
Period B	15th May to 31st July	1st April
Period C	1st November to 15th December	1st October

These dates will apply from 1st January 1999 until further notice

- Please fill in the form giving your name, address and phone number. Please tick the type and level of exam, along with the period and year. Finally, fill in the fee box with the appropriate amount. You should send this form with a cheque or postal order to: **Rockschool, Broomfield House, 10 Broomfield Road, Richmond, Surrey TW9 3HS.**

- When you enter an exam you will receive from Rockschool an acknowledgement letter containing your exam entry number along with a copy of our exam regulations.

- Rockschool will allocate your entry to a centre and you will receive notification of the exam, showing a date, location and time as well as advice of what to bring to the centre.

- You should inform Rockschool of any cancellations or alterations to the schedule as soon as you can as it is usually not possible to transfer entries from one centre, or one period, to another without the payment of an additional fee.

- Please bring your music book and CD to the exam. You may not use photocopied music, nor the music used by someone else in another exam. The examiner will stamp each book after each session. You may be barred from taking an exam if you use someone else's music.

- You should aim to arrive for your *Drums* Grade 5 exam fifteen minutes before the time stated on the schedule.

- The exam centre will have a waiting area and warm-up facilities which you may use prior to being called into the main exam room.

- Each Rockschool Grade exam and *Performer Zone* Performance Certificate is scheduled to last for 25 minutes. The *Performer Zone* Band Exam will last 30 minutes. You can use a small proportion of this time to warm up and get ready.

- About 2 to 3 weeks after the exam you will receive a typed copy of the examiner's mark sheet. Every successful performer will receive a Rockschool certificate of achievement.